TO THE RESCUE!

Police

to the Rescue
Around the World

Linda Staniford

raintree

a Capstone company — publishers for children

Raintree is an imprint of Capstone Global Library Limited, a company incorporated in England and Wales having its registered office at 264 Banbury Road, Oxford OX2 7DY – Registered company number: 6695582

www.raintree.co.uk
myorders@raintree.co.uk

Edited by Linda Staniford
Designed by Steve Mead
Picture research by Eric Gohl
Production by Aileen Taylor
Originated by Capstone Global Library Ltd
Printed and bound in China

ISBN 978 1 474 71522 5
19 18 17 16 15
10 9 8 7 6 5 4 3 2 1

British Library Cataloguing in Publication Data
A full catalogue record for this book is available from the British Library.

Acknowledgements
We would like to thank the following for permission to reproduce photographs:
Alamy: Agencja Fotograficzna Caro, 10, 22 (middle), Eric Nathan, 9, ZUMA Press, Inc, 21; AP Photo: Imaginechina, 20, Toby Talbot, 13, 22 (top); Getty Images: Cameron Spencer, 14; iStockphoto: tirc83, 7, Yuri_Arcurs, 5; Newscom: EPA/Massimo Percossi, 17, KRT/Mandi Wright, 19, 22 (bottom), REX/Per Lindgren, 16, ZUMA Press/Taylor Weidman, 15; Shutterstock: AFNR, 11, arindambanerjee, 8, EJMzagsfan, cover, pcruciatti, 4, Phil McDonald, 18, back cover (right), sdecoret, 6, VanderWolf Images, 12, back cover (left)

Design Elements: Shutterstock

Every effort has been made to contact copyright holders of material reproduced in this book. Any omissions will be rectified in subsequent printings if notice is given to the publisher.

Contents

Some words are shown in bold, **like this**. You can find out what they mean by looking in the glossary.

What do the police do?

The police come to the rescue to keep us safe. All over the world, they stop people breaking laws and committing crimes.

When someone commits a crime, the police try to catch that person. They also help people who have been hurt when a crime is committed.

How do the police keep us safe?

Every country in the world has laws. Laws are like rules and they are meant to keep us safe.

If someone breaks a law they may cause **damage** or hurt other people. The police make sure that people do not break the laws of the country they live in.

What do the police wear?

Police officers wear a **uniform** with a hat or helmet. They may wear special **body armour** that protects them from **injury**.

In India, where it is often hot, police wear light coloured uniforms with short sleeves. In Russia, where it can be very cold, they wear thick coats and warm hats.

What do the police carry?

Police carry a radio so that they can contact each other quickly. They have handcuffs for when they catch a **criminal.**

Some police officers carry weapons. Sometimes they have to carry riot shields. These stop them getting injured by crowds.

How do the police travel?

Police officers drive specially marked cars or motorbikes. The cars and bikes have loud sirens and flashing lights.

In Russia, it can be very cold and snowy. Police cannot use cars where there is deep snow, so they travel by **snowmobile**.

How do the police rescue people?

In Australia, some people live far away from towns and cities. If they get lost or injured, the police use a helicopter to rescue them.

In Nepal, there was a huge **earthquake.**
The ground shook and buildings
collapsed. Police helped rescue people
who were trapped underneath the rubble.

What are water police?

In Venice, people travel on **canals** instead of on roads. The police use boats or jet skis to travel to where they are needed.

Police divers search underwater for injured people or **evidence** of crimes. When a big ship was wrecked in the sea near Italy, police divers helped rescue passengers.

Do the police use animals?

The police ride horses at events where there are large crowds of people. The Canadian Mounted Police are famous for using horses in their work.

Dogs have a very good sense of smell. They can even smell weapons in people's bags. This dog is being used to search for weapons at an airport.

Making the world a safer place!

Police often visit schools and communities. They talk about how we can stay safe in our homes and on the streets.

The police are very brave people. It is good to know we can call them if there is an **emergency**. But it is also important to know how to keep ourselves safe.

Quiz

Question 1
What kind of transport do police often use in Russia?
a) snowmobile
b) helicopter
c) horses

Question 2
Which of these would a police officer usually carry?
a) a shopping bag
b) a radio
c) a library book

Question 3
What do the police use dogs for?
a) to find their lunch
b) to keep them company
c) to find hidden weapons at airports

Answers: 1a), 2b), 3c)

Glossary

body armour protective clothing worn to prevent injury to the body

canal human-made waterway

collapse fall down suddenly; buildings often collapse during earthquakes

criminal someone who breaks the law

damage injury or harm

earthquake very strong shaking or trembling of the ground

emergency sudden and dangerous situation that must be handled quickly

evidence information, items, and facts that help prove something is true or false

injury damage to a part of the body

snowmobile a vehicle with an engine and skis or runners; snowmobiles travel over snow

uniform special clothes that members of a particular group wear

Find out more

Books

First Book of Emergency Vehicles, Isabel Thomas (A&C Black, 2014)

In an Emergency: Call the Police, Cath Senker (Franklin Watts, 2013)

People who Help Us: Police, Honor Head (Wayland, 2012)

Police Officer: People who Help Us, Rebecca Hunter (Tulip Books, 2014)

Websites

More information about what the police do:

http://easyscienceforkids.com/all-about-police-dogs/

http://www.factmonster.com/ipka/A0934715.html

http://www.squizzes.com/police-fast-facts

Index